GIANTS OF THE OLD TESTAMENT

LESSONS ON LIVING FROM
ELIJAH

A devotional by
WOODROW KROLL

Back to the Bible®

ELIJAH
published by Back to the Bible
©1998 by Woodrow Kroll

International Standard Book Number
0-8474-0686-5

Edited by Rachel Derowitsch
Cover design by Robert Greuter
& Associates

Unless otherwise noted, all Scripture is taken from The New King James Version. Copyright © 1979, 1980, 1982, Thomas Nelson, Inc.
Used by permission.

ALL RIGHTS RESERVED
No part of this publication may be reproduced, stored in a retrieval system or transmitted, in any form or by any means—electronic, mechanical photocopying, recording or otherwise—except for brief quotations in printed reviews or articles, without the prior written permission of the publisher.

For information:
BACK TO THE BIBLE
POST OFFICE BOX 82808
LINCOLN, NEBRASKA 68501

1 2 3 4 5 6 7 8—04 03 02 01 00 99 98

Printed in the USA

CONTENTS

Day 1	On Ravens' Wings	4
Day 2	When the Creek Dries Up	6
Day 3	Me First?	8
Day 4	Fervent Prayer	10
Day 5	Go and Tell!	12
Day 6	Is That You, O Troubler?	14
Day 7	Faltering Between	16
Day 8	The God Who Answers	18
Day 9	Empty Gods	20
Day 10	Confident Praying	22
Day 11	Always Complete	24
Day 12	A Sure Expectation	26
Day 13	Seven Times Praying	28
Day 14	The Powerful Hand of the Lord	30
Day 15	Foolish Fears	32
Day 16	Is It Enough?	34
Day 17	Arise and Eat	36
Day 18	Strength for the Journey	38
Day 19	What Are You Doing Here?	40
Day 20	I Alone Am Left	42
Day 21	Blessed Quietness	44
Day 22	Face Your Fears	46
Day 23	All Is Not Lost	48
Day 24	No Turning Back	50
Day 25	Blessed Enemy	52
Day 26	Is There No God?	54
Day 27	God Takes Care of His Own	56
Day 28	Step-by-step	58
Day 29	Let Your Light Still Shine	60
Day 30	In the Midst of the Whirlwind	62
Day 31	In His Steps	64

DAY 1

1 Kings 17:2-5

Then the word of the L<small>ORD</small> came to him, saying, "Get away from here and turn eastward, and hide by the Brook Cherith, which flows into the Jordan. And it will be that you shall drink from the brook, and I have commanded the ravens to feed you there." So he went and did according to the word of the L<small>ORD</small>, for he went and stayed by the Brook Cherith, which flows into the Jordan.

On Ravens' Wings

A man wanted to buy a Rolls Royce. After thinking about it for several months, he contacted the automobile dealership to gather the pertinent facts about the model he was considering buying. He found out the price and then proceeded with some thorough questions about the automobile. Finally, only one question remained unanswered: "What is the horsepower of this engine?" The salesman couldn't find that information in the brochures. Not knowing where else to look, he appealed to his sales manager, and the manager cabled the home office in England. The answer came back with just one word: "Adequate."

After Elijah confronted King Ahab, God ordered him to go into hiding. The place chosen, the Brook Cherith, was a great place to hide. Ahab would never think of looking in such a forsaken area, but it was a challenge to survive there. Yet God proved Himself adequate. There was a brook for water, and at His command even the ravens helped provide for Elijah's needs.

No situation or circumstance is too difficult for God. When the world withholds its provision, He is adequate. What God uses to provide for you may seem strange, but with all of creation willing to do His bidding, He will find a way.

Take heart. Those dark shadows on the horizon may well be God's ravens. Be assured that God will never forsake you nor fail you. Whatever your circumstances, you will always find Him adequate.

Others may fail you, but God never will.

Reflections/Prayer Requests

DAY 2

1 Kings 17:6-7

The ravens brought him bread and meat in the morning, and bread and meat in the evening; and he drank from the brook. And it happened after a while that the brook dried up, because there had been no rain in the land.

When the Creek Dries Up

John Brenz, a friend of Martin Luther, was hated by Emperor Charles V. He often tried to kill Brenz and on one occasion sent a troop of cavalrymen to arrest him. Hearing about the plot, Brenz took a loaf of bread and went to a nearby town, where he hid in a hayloft. He was there for 14 days. Obviously one loaf of bread was not enough for two weeks. But each day a hen came into the loft and laid an egg without cackling. In this way the Lord kept John Brenz alive. On the 15th day the hen did not show up. It seemed like the one lifeline he had clung to had been severed. As he was wondering what he would do without food, John heard the people in the streets below say, "The cavalrymen are gone at last!"

Elijah also experienced what appeared to be the loss of an essential lifeline. God had sent him out into the wilderness and provided food through the ministry of ravens and water from a small creek. But then a difficult situation became worse. As the drought continued, the brook dried up. At first glance, it might seem that God no longer cared about what happened to His prophet. Instead, God chose to provide in a different way and graciously directed him to the home of a widow in the city of Zarephath (v. 9).

Perhaps you feel that your creek also has dried up. The friend who has been your source of refreshment in a spiritual desert has moved away. The person who has been your lifeline at work has taken a new job. Whatever the case, trust God to provide through another source. It may be far different from what met your need before, but remember, God will not fail you.

When God closes a door, He always opens a window.

Reflections/Prayer Requests

_____
_____
_____
_____
_____
_____
_____
_____

DAY 3

1 Kings 17:13-15

And Elijah said to her, "Do not fear; go and do as you have said, but make me a small cake from it first, and bring it to me; and afterward make some for yourself and your son. For thus says the LORD God of Israel: 'The bin of flour shall not be used up, nor shall the jar of oil run dry, until the day the LORD sends rain on the earth.'" So she went away and did according to the word of Elijah; and she and he and her household ate for many days.

Me First?

Our actions say a lot about our priorities. A woman married to a baseball coach for 34 years began to suspect that perhaps baseball meant more to him than she did. One particularly frustrating day, she decided to test his priorities and see if her suspicions were true. She asked, "Frank, would you miss my funeral to go to a ball game?" Calmly, her husband replied, "Roberta, what makes you think I'd schedule your funeral on the day of a game?"

Elijah was sent to stay with a widow in Zarephath. But before he entrusted himself to her, he wanted to know her priorities. The test was very simple. In the midst of dire need, he instructed her to make a small cake from her meager supplies and bring it to him *first*. By her actions she would reveal her priorities; by her priorities she would reveal her trust in God. Based on her gracious response, it's obvious that she passed with flying colors.

It's easy to do the right thing when there is enough for all. But that is not a good test of our priorities. Our true priorities become apparent when we're forced to make a sacrificial choice. No matter what we profess, our actions will confirm or deny whether we're able to trust the Lord in the face of need.

What do your actions say about your priorities? What do your priorities say about your trust in God? Are you able to trust the Lord and put others first? When you have your priorities straight, God takes care of the rest.

Actions are based on priorities and priorities are based on faith.

Reflections/Prayer Requests

DAY 4

1 Kings 17:20-22

Then he cried out to the L̲o̲r̲d̲ and said, "O L̲o̲r̲d̲ my God, have You also brought tragedy on the widow with whom I lodge, by killing her son?" And he stretched himself out on the child three times, and cried out to the L̲o̲r̲d̲ and said, "O L̲o̲r̲d̲ my God, I pray, let this child's soul come back to him." Then the L̲o̲r̲d̲ heard the voice of Elijah; and the soul of the child came back to him, and he revived.

Fervent Prayer

E. M. Bounds wrote, "What the Church needs today is not more machinery or better, not new organizations or more novel methods, but men whom the Holy Spirit can use—men of prayer, men mighty in prayer."

Elijah was such a man. When faced with a major crisis—the death of a young boy, the only child of a widow who had shown him much kindness—he immediately resorted to the most potent power he knew: prayer. Without hesitation, he cast himself upon the mercy of God and cried out for His grace to be extended to this young man and his widowed mother. With passion Elijah entreated the Lord, and He answered. It is no surprise, then, that when the apostle James looked for an example of fervent prayer, he chose Elijah

(James 5:16-17). The prophet was a man mighty in prayer because he was fervent in prayer.

Too often Christians petition God with room-temperature prayers. They convey the facts, but they lack the fervor. They are sincere, but they don't sizzle. The same men and women who yell themselves hoarse at a sporting event become reluctant to raise their voice when speaking to God. Yet they expect an enthusiastic response from God to their halfhearted requests.

Find a time and place today where you can pour out your heart to God. Don't fake your emotions, but pray for those needs that have a strong grip on your spirit. If you have none, ask God to give you some. Let your approach to God reflect the urgency and the ardor of your concerns.

Fervent prayers produce phenomenal results.

Reflections/Prayer Requests

_____

_____

_____

_____

_____

_____

DAY 5

1 Kings 18:7-8

Now as Obadiah was on his way, suddenly Elijah met him; and he recognized him, and fell on his face, and said, "Is that you, my lord Elijah?" And he answered him, "It is I. Go, tell your master, 'Elijah is here.'"

Go and Tell!

Many years ago there was a great missionary rally held in the Royal Albert Hall in London, England. The Duke of Wellington was there, the man who had defeated the armies of Napoleon Bonaparte. A clergyman turned to him and asked, "My Lord Duke, do you believe in missions?" The duke replied, "What are your marching orders?" The man responded, "Well, of course, the Bible says we're to go into all the world." "Then," said the duke, "you have nothing to say about it. As a soldier, you're simply to obey orders."

When Obadiah met Elijah, he, too, received marching orders. Elijah spoke as from the Lord when he said, "Go and tell." "Go to your master, Ahab, one of the most godless kings who ever ruled Israel, and tell him that the spokesman for God is back in the land." This was not a suggestion; it was not a recommendation; it was a command. Obadiah was afraid. He said, "Are you sending me to my death? If I go and tell Ahab you're here and you disappear on me, Ahab will kill me." But in spite of his fears, Obadiah obeyed.

When Christ met His disciples after the resurrection, He gave the same orders. Go! "Go therefore and make disciples" (Matt. 28:19). Tell! "Teaching them to observe all things" (v. 20). These, too, are not open for discussion. We may have our fears, but Christ's commands are our marching orders.

Are you willing to "go and tell"? Perhaps it's "go and tell" your next-door neighbor, or someone at work or maybe even someone who lives halfway around the world. Whatever the case, obedience to the Lord is the only way to handle your fears. When we trust and obey, God has a way of taking care of our fears. Our orders are clear: Go and tell!

When it comes to God's commands, the issue is not clarity; it's commitment.

Reflections/Prayer Requests

_____
_____
_____
_____
_____

DAY 6

1 Kings 18:17-18

Then it happened, when Ahab saw Elijah, that Ahab said to him, "Is that you, O troubler of Israel?" And he answered, "I have not troubled Israel, but you and your father's house have, in that you have forsaken the commandments of the LORD and you have followed the Baals."

Is That You, O Troubler?

A well-known professional golfer was playing in a tournament with then-president Gerald Ford, fellow pro Jack Nicklaus and Billy Graham. After the round was over, one of the other pros on the tour asked, "Hey, what was it like playing with the president and Billy Graham?" The pro said with disgust, "I don't need Billy Graham stuffing religion down my throat!" With that he headed for the practice tee. His friend followed, and after the golfer had pounded out his fury on a bucket of golf balls, he asked, "Was Billy a little rough on you out there?" The pro sighed and said with embarrassment, "No, he didn't even mention religion."

Elijah found himself in the same situation. Without even opening his mouth, the prophet found himself accused by Ahab as a "troubler." The accusation was obviously false. It was Ahab who was Israel's true troubler. His sin and the sin of those who had gone before him were the cause of God's judgment on Israel. But it was easier for Ahab to place the blame for his uneasy conscience on someone else than to face the truth about himself.

The world is always looking for someone to blame, isn't it? And Christians are a convenient target. We Christians are different (which make us suspect to start with), and the witness of our lives can be very convicting even when we say nothing. No wonder Christians have borne the brunt of persecution from the time of Nero to the present.

Don't be surprised or dismayed if you are being persecuted, in whatever form it may take. Consider it a confirmation that Christ is obviously within you and radiating from you.

Jesus Christ is both a comfort for Christians and an irritation for the world.

Reflections/Prayer Requests

_____

_____

_____

_____

_____

DAY 7

1 Kings 18:21

And Elijah came to all the people, and said, "How long will you falter between two opinions? If the LORD is God, follow Him; but if Baal, then follow him." But the people answered him not a word.

Faltering Between

A few years ago, *USA Today* carried the news that the Procrastinators Club was planning to form a political party, possibly in time for the November elections. "Our party will be the most harmonious of all the political parties," said club president Les Waas. "If we ever disagree on an issue, we'll never get around to discussing it." Waas, an expert at public speaking, said with tongue in cheek that the Procrastinator Party would like to hold its nominating convention by the first week in November. "If we don't get it done until the second week, we might ask the authorities to move the election back a couple of weeks to accommodate us."

The people of Elijah's day were procrastinators as well. The prophet confronted them with an important decision. Would they follow the Lord, or would they follow Baal? Their response to such an ultimatum, however, was to stall. They refused to answer.

Some things can be put off with no ultimate harm. If we don't get our strawberries planted this year, there's always next year. If we fail to get around to reading this year's best-sellers, a new list of them will be available in the future. But the same can't be said for our spiritual lives. The spiritual choices we fail to make will haunt us for eternity.

Are you procrastinating when it comes to reading your Bible? Have you put off spending time in prayer? Is it possible you have never gotten around to trusting Jesus Christ as your personal Savior? If so, stop "faltering" and start making the spiritual decisions that will make a difference for eternity. No one else can make these decisions for you. Make them today!

Not to decide is to decide.

Reflections/Prayer Requests

_____
_____
_____
_____
_____
_____
_____
_____

DAY 8

1 Kings 18:24

"Then you call on the name of your gods, and I will call on the name of the LORD; and the God who answers by fire, He is God." So all the people answered and said, "It is well spoken."

The God Who Answers

A magazine cartoon showed a little fellow kneeling beside his bed for his bedtime prayers. He was saying with some measure of disgust, "Uncle Jim still doesn't have a job; Sis still doesn't have a date for the prom; Grandma is still feeling poorly—and I'm tired of praying for this family and not getting results." Admittedly, it would be discouraging to think that God doesn't answer our prayers.

But Elijah had no such doubts. If God is truly God, He will answer. And his confidence was well rewarded. Not only did God answer, but He answered in such a dramatic way that the people could no longer question who was really God. Even the things that don't normally burn, the stones and the dust, were consumed when God answered by fire (v. 38). In an unmistakable way, the Lord responded to Elijah's prayer.

The distinguishing mark of the Christian faith is that we have a living God who not only hears but answers our prayers. His ear and His heart are both attuned to our cry. His answers may not come at the time we want them, but they will come at the time when they will do the most good. He does not always answer in the way we expect, but He will always answer in the way that's best for us.

It's not always easy to trust God for the right answer at the right time, but it's always best. Our confident assurance is that if we ask according to His will, "we know that we have the petitions that we have asked of Him" (1 John 5:15).

Do not grow weary in your prayers. Seek to know God's will and then confidently pray for His response. The God who hears will also answer—at the right time and in the right way.

The prayer is up to us; the answer is up to God.

Reflections/Prayer Requests

_____

_____

_____

_____

_____

_____

_____

DAY 9

1 Kings 18:27-29

And so it was, at noon, that Elijah mocked them and said, "Cry aloud, for he is a god; either he is meditating, or he is busy, or he is on a journey, or perhaps he is sleeping and must be awakened." So they cried aloud, and cut themselves, as was their custom, with knives and lances, until the blood gushed out on them. And it was so, when midday was past, that they prophesied until the time of the offering of the evening sacrifice. But there was no voice; no one answered, no one paid attention.

Empty Gods

Ralph Barton was a successful cartoonist. But he chose to end his life, leaving a note that read: "I have had few difficulties, many friends, great successes. I have gone from wife to wife, and from house to house, and visited great countries of the world; but I am fed up with inventing devices to fill up twenty-four hours of the day." How tragic! Like Ralph Barton, when we place our faith in things that are empty, the consequences are severe.

The prophets of Baal discovered this as well. They were sincere to the point of frenzy in their worship, but to no avail. Elijah mocked them, but he also pointed out an important truth—nobody was home. There was no voice, no answer, no god to pay attention to their pleas. Their religion was empty. And ultimately it caused their death (v. 40).

Everything the world offers is likewise empty. The money, the fame, the "good times" cannot fill the void in our lives because they have no substance. They seem real when we casually observe them, but the moment the stresses of life hit, they dissolve like cotton candy. Eventually, they also lead to our death—eternal separation from the Father. Don't make the same mistake the prophets of Baal did; make sure that what you put first in your life is real.

Give thanks today that you can know that Jesus is real. His resurrection proves that there is substance to His claims. When you grasp Him, you never have to worry about coming up empty-handed. Latch onto the eternal; latch onto Jesus Christ as your Lord and Savior.

If your life is empty, fill it with Christ.

Reflections/Prayer Requests

_____

_____

_____

_____

_____

DAY 10

1 Kings 18:33-35

And he put the wood in order, cut the bull in pieces, and laid it on the wood, and said, "Fill four waterpots with water, and pour it on the burnt sacrifice and on the wood." Then he said, "Do it a second time," and they did it a second time; and he said, "Do it a third time," and they did it a third time. So the water ran all around the altar; and he also filled the trench with water.

Confident Praying

In the early days of our country, a traveler came to the banks of the Mississippi River. There was no bridge but it was early winter, and the surface of the river was covered with ice. He had no way of knowing, however, if the ice could bear his weight. Finally, after much hesitation and with many fears, he began to creep cautiously across the ice on his hands and knees. As he was about halfway across the river, he heard the sound of singing behind him. Looking back, he saw a man driving a horse-drawn load of coal across the ice. Here the traveler was—trembling, afraid the ice was not strong enough to bear him—and there came this man, his horses, his sleigh and his load of coal, confidently upheld by the same ice!

When it came time for God to respond to Elijah's prayer, Elijah demonstrated his confidence in God. He didn't simply build an altar and call down fire. Instead, three times he drenched the altar and the sacrifice with water until everything was saturated. Then he filled the trench around the altar with water as well. He was sure that God would not only answer, but answer in a powerful way.

Christians can have this same confidence. If we pray according to God's will, we have the assurance that God will answer, no matter how difficult our circumstances (John 14:14).

Is there something in your life that you've not prayed about because you fear it is impossible? Come to God with confidence. Remember, with God all things are possible—so pray accordingly.

Be confident; God is able.

Reflections/Prayer Requests

_____

_____

_____

_____

_____

_____

_____

DAY 11

1 Kings 18:38-39

Then the fire of the Lord fell and consumed the burnt sacrifice, and the wood and the stones and the dust, and it licked up the water that was in the trench. Now when all the people saw it, they fell on their faces; and they said, "The Lord, He is God! The Lord, He is God!"

Always Complete

Often the little things in life trip us up. A tragic example is an Eastern Airlines jumbo jet that crashed in the Everglades of Florida. The plane, Flight 401, was bound from New York to Miami with a heavy load of holiday passengers. As the plane approached the Miami airport for its landing, the indicator that verifies the proper deployment of the landing gear failed to light. The plane flew in a large circle over the swamps of the Everglades while the cockpit crew checked to see if the gear actually had not deployed, or if the bulb in the signal light was defective. When the flight engineer tried to remove the light bulb, it wouldn't budge. The other members of the crew tried to help him. As they struggled with the bulb, no one noticed the aircraft was losing altitude, and the plane simply flew into the swamp. Many people lost their lives in the crash.

Contrast this human failure with the God who answers by fire. He never misses a detail. When Elijah prayed, God answered so completely and fully that the people could only cry out, "The Lord, He is God!" So thorough was the Lord's response that even the stones and the dust were consumed. Nothing related to Elijah's sacrifice—the wood, the stones, the dust, the bulls—was left untouched. The God who answers by fire is the God of completeness.

When you pray, trust God for the particulars. You can be sure that He will never overlook anything that is necessary for your spiritual well-being. No piece of minutia will escape His attention. Give Him the total control of your life, bathe it in prayer, but leave the details to God.

With God, no problem is too big and no detail is too small.

Reflections/Prayer Requests

_____
_____
_____
_____
_____
_____
_____

DAY 12

1 Kings 18:41-42

Then Elijah said to Ahab, "Go up, eat and drink; for there is the sound of abundance of rain." So Ahab went up to eat and drink. And Elijah went up to the top of Carmel; then he bowed down on the ground, and put his face between his knees.

A Sure Expectation

There had been a drought for weeks in a Midwest farming community, so some farmers arranged to gather in a little prairie church and plead for rain. The day appointed for their small church to pray dawned cloudless, with no sign of rain. The people gathered and the pastor approached the pulpit. Looking over the congregation, however, he announced that they would have a benediction and go home. The deacons were quite upset and confronted the pastor after the service. "Why are you sending us home without praying for rain?" they wanted to know. "Simple enough," replied the pastor. "You obviously aren't expecting God to answer. None of you brought an umbrella."

Elijah not only prayed, but he expected an answer. Before the clouds formed or the thunder boomed, he heard the "sound of abundance of rain." He knew that he was praying according to the will of God and he was confident, before any external evidence could confirm his faith, that God would supply the rain He promised. Elijah's command to Ahab was based on the assurance of God's answer, not the whims of nature.

The Bible tells us to pray without doubting (James 1:6). When we come to God, knowing that we are asking according to His will, we don't have to be intimidated by our circumstances. We can have the confidence that when the time is right, God will answer. We need to act according to His promised answer, not according to our fearful uncertainties.

As you pray, don't look around you; look above you. Real answers to prayer don't come from the situations we find ourselves in. Real answers come from our Heavenly Father.

Pray according to faith, not circumstances.

Reflections/Prayer Requests

_____

_____

_____

_____

_____

_____

DAY 13

1 Kings 18:42-44

So Ahab went up to eat and drink. And Elijah went up to the top of Carmel; then he bowed down on the ground, and put his face between his knees, and said to his servant, "Go up now, look toward the sea." So he went up and looked, and said, "There is nothing." And seven times he said, "Go again." Then it came to pass the seventh time, that he said, "There is a cloud, as small as a man's hand, rising out of the sea!"

Seven Times Praying

Concerning answers to prayer George Mueller wrote, "Never give up until the answer comes. I have been praying every day for 52 years for two men, sons of a friend of my youth. They are not converted yet, but they will be! . . . The great fault of the children of God is that they do not continue in prayer; they do not go on praying; they do not persevere. If they desire anything for God's glory, they should pray until they get it."

Elijah believed in persistent praying. Seven times he bowed in prayer; seven times he sent his servant to see if God had answered yet. While there is nothing magical about the number seven, it is the number associated with completeness in the Bible. When this seventh prayer was offered, the servant came back with the report that a cloud was on the horizon. Elijah kept praying until his prayer was completed.

A prayer is never complete until God has answered. We need to keep praying until we have the assurance in our hearts that God's answer has been given or is on the way. To stop praying too soon may forfeit the very thing we're praying for.

Don't be a quitter. Keep on with your prayers until they're complete. Let God's answer be your final amen! Oh, those two men for whom George Mueller prayed for so long? One became a Christian at Mueller's funeral; the other some years later. Keep on praying.

Prayer is never complete until God has answered.

Reflections/Prayer Requests

_____

_____

_____

_____

_____

_____

_____

_____

DAY 14

1 Kings 18:45-46

Now it happened in the meantime that the sky became black with clouds and wind, and there was a heavy rain. So Ahab rode away and went to Jezreel. Then the hand of the LORD came upon Elijah; and he girded up his loins and ran ahead of Ahab to the entrance of Jezreel.

The Powerful Hand of the Lord

For skiers, the problem is not swooshing downhill with the thrill of speed and precision. It's going back uphill again. That's why ski lifts were invented. But now a new ski innovation has been introduced to the world of downhill skiing. Known as ski sailing, it enables a skier with the aid of a sail, or parachute-type device, to ski uphill using the power of the wind. By virtue of the wind, the power behind you becomes greater than the hill above you.

Elijah also knew what it was like to experience a power beyond himself to accomplish what God required. As the rains descended, it became a race to see who would first arrive back at Jezreel to announce the news of Baal's defeat. It was not under his own power, but by "the hand of the Lord" that Elijah outdistanced Ahab, even though the king had a horse and chariot and Elijah was on foot.

When confronted with difficult tasks, we often hesitate because we fail to take into account the divine power we have behind us. When God's hand is upon us, no challenge is too great for us. Others may have advantages we don't possess. They may be more experienced, more knowledgeable or more talented, but all of that is irrelevant if God's hand is upon us. Human resources are no match for God's power.

If you are disadvantaged today, facing difficulties beyond your abilities, don't give up. Ask God to apply His powerful hand to your situation. With the power of God filling your sails, no slope is too steep. Others may appear to have the upper hand, but God has the more powerful hand.

If your life is an uphill slope, set your sails to catch God's power.

Reflections/Prayer Requests

_____

_____

_____

_____

_____

_____

_____

DAY 15

1 Kings 19:1-3

And Ahab told Jezebel all that Elijah had done, also how he had executed all the prophets with the sword. Then Jezebel sent a messenger to Elijah, saying, "So let the gods do to me, and more also, if I do not make your life as the life of one of them by tomorrow about this time." And when he saw that, he arose and ran for his life, and went to Beersheba, which belongs to Judah, and left his servant there.

Foolish Fears

Unfounded fear can cause us great harm. Vance Havner used to tell the story of a man who accidentally wandered into a cemetery one night. When he realized where he was, he got out of there in record time, stumbling over tombstones, falling down and scratching himself in the bushes. The next morning someone asked him, "Don't you know that ghosts can't hurt you?" "I know that," he replied, "but they can sure make you hurt yourself."

Like the man's in the cemetery, Elijah's fears were also unfounded. The same God who kept him safe in the midst of 450 prophets of Baal was certainly able to protect him from the wrath of the wicked Queen Jezebel. Yet his fears caused him to compromise his testimony and prevented

God from demonstrating His power against wickedness in high places. Instead of trusting God to protect him, Elijah fled into the wilderness. How foolish!

Did you know that fear is one of the major causes for disobedience among Christians? God's Word is filled with promises of His provision (Phil. 4:19) and our protection (Ps. 91). Yet we often fail to accomplish God's will because we are afraid that we will be physically harmed or financially humbled in the process. This is foolish as well.

Are you facing fear today? Perhaps you are afraid of losing your job, of developing cancer or being left by your spouse. At times all of us experience fear. But don't allow fear to keep you from being used by God. He has kept you thus far; trust Him for the rest of the way.

The only known antidote to fear is faith.

Reflections/Prayer Requests

_____
_____
_____
_____
_____
_____

DAY 16

1 Kings 19:4

But he himself went a day's journey into the wilderness, and came and sat down under a broom tree. And he prayed that he might die, and said, "It is enough! Now, LORD, take my life, for I am no better than my fathers!"

Is It Enough?

George Sweeting related that the famous Dutch artist Vincent van Gogh once felt called to be an evangelist. He had grown up in a Christian home and in 1878, at the age of 24, enrolled in a school for evangelism in Brussels. After graduating, he preached for a year. Then for reasons unknown, van Gogh forsook his call. In 1889 he began to paint like a driven man, finishing 200 paintings in two years. Then at age 37, confused, impoverished and ill, he borrowed a gun and ended his life. He decided he had had enough.

Elijah, too, reached the point in his life when he felt it was enough. Rather than commit suicide, however, he asked God to take his life. But God had other plans for Elijah. He knew that some of the prophet's greatest successes still lay ahead of him: anointing the king of Syria and the king of Israel, training Elisha as his successor, and miraculously crossing the Jordan on a dry river bed. Instead of taking his life,

God strengthened him and sent Elijah back to active duty.

I don't believe suicide causes a Christian to lose his salvation, but it clearly cuts short the service a believer can offer to the Lord. Since our rewards in heaven are based on the deeds of our lives right now (2 Cor. 5:10), all missed opportunities will mean an eternal loss that cannot be made up. Therefore, while life may become discouraging, it is always too soon to say, "Enough!"

Perhaps you feel like saying, "It is enough!" If not tempted to take your life, you may at least feel like you no longer want to walk with the Lord. God understands, and if you place your life completely in His loving hands, He can give you the grace to start over. Who knows? God may have the most productive years of your life planned for your future.

Our quitting point is God's beginning point.

Reflections/Prayer Requests

_____

_____

_____

_____

_____

DAY 17

1 Kings 19:5-6

Then as he lay and slept under a broom tree, suddenly an angel touched him, and said to him, "Arise and eat." Then he looked, and there by his head was a cake baked on coals, and a jar of water. So he ate and drank, and lay down again.

Arise and Eat

A missionary passed a field where lepers were at work. He noticed two in particular who were sowing peas. Because of their disease, one had no hands and the other had no feet. The one who lacked hands, however, was carrying upon his back the other who had no feet. He, in turn, carried the bag of seed and dropped a pea every now and then, which the other pressed into the ground with his feet. Together they got the job done, something neither could do by himself.

Elijah was equally pressed into cooperation with an angel of the Lord. The angel provided food and water, but it was Elijah who had to "arise and eat." While God made sure that Elijah received what he lacked, He was not about to spoon-feed the prophet. Elijah had to eat for himself. It was when he worked together with the angel, each doing his part, that Elijah received the nourishment and strength he needed for the task before him.

Christians tend to fall into one of two extremes: either we expect God to do it all, or we feel like the whole load is on our shoulders and we burn out trying to do more than we should. In reality, the Christian life is a matter of cooperation. As God's Spirit works to produce Christ's character in our lives, we work to allow that character to be reflected in the things we say and do. Together we bring glory to the Father.

Take a few moments to reflect on your Christian life. Are you trying to do it all? Are you sitting back and expecting God to do everything? Or are you working together with the Holy Spirit to accomplish in and through you the will of your Heavenly Father? Remember, God provides, but we "arise and eat."

What God supplies, we must apply.

Reflections/Prayer Requests

_____
_____
_____
_____
_____
_____
_____
_____

DAY 18

1 Kings 19:8

*So he arose, and ate and drank;
and he went in the strength
of that food forty days and forty nights
as far as Horeb, the mountain of God.*

Strength for the Journey

One New Year's Day in the Tournament of Roses parade, a beautiful float suddenly sputtered and quit. After checking for mechanical problems, the crew discovered that the vehicle pulling the float was simply out of fuel. The whole parade was held up until someone could get a can of gasoline. The most amusing thing about this whole fiasco was that the float represented the Standard Oil Company. With its vast oil resources, its truck ran out of gas!

Elijah had run out of gas as well. He had victoriously confronted the prophets of Baal and revived the people of Israel (1 Kings 18:20-40). He had raced King Ahab back to Jezreel and won (v. 46). Then he had fled from the wrath of Queen Jezebel and gone a day's journey into the wilderness (19:1-3). Now he was faced with another journey, this time to meet with God on Mount Horeb, but he didn't have the strength to do it on his own. God sent an angel of the Lord, who said to Elijah, "The journey is too great for you"

(v. 7). Then God gave Elijah supernatural strength, and in that strength he traveled for 40 days and 40 nights.

Believers are not able to live the victorious Christian life on their own strength either. God knows that. But He is also able to give us the strength we need. The apostle Paul said, "I can do all things through Christ who strengthens me" (Phil. 4:13). God has unlimited resources, but unless we appropriate them to our lives, they do us no good.

Don't settle for a stalled-out Christian life. While you are inadequate in yourself, God is more than sufficient for all your needs. Call on Him today and you'll experience all the strength you need for the journey.

Be filled with the Spirit and you'll never run out of gas.

Reflections/Prayer Requests

_____
_____
_____
_____
_____
_____
_____

DAY 19

1 Kings 19:9

And there he went into a cave, and spent the night in that place; and behold, the word of the LORD came to him, and He said to him, "What are you doing here, Elijah?"

What Are You Doing Here?

A woman named Maria stopped by Back to the Bible and asked for a tour. While she was waiting in the lobby, she spoke with a member of our staff for a few minutes. She shared that she used to be a power broker on Wall Street and mingled with Donald Trump and Ronald Reagan and folks like that. But when she became a believer, she realized that there is more to living than just "making a living." Now she owns a fishing lodge in northern Minnesota. She spends her days canoeing, reading and helping her visitors to relax. She wants to develop her lodge into a retreat center for pastors and other Christians. She concluded, "This is the ministry God has called me to."

On Mount Horeb, God confronted Elijah with his ministry as well. When God asked him, "What are you doing here?" He knew the answer. He knew that Elijah had fled his responsibilities and left behind his ministry. But He wanted Elijah to realize that too. God's question was designed to cause Elijah to think about his ultimate purpose in life.

All Christians need to ask themselves, "What am I doing here? Why am I alive? What does God have for me to do?" There is no believer who does not have a God-given purpose for his life. In fact, God designs each of us with a specific purpose in mind. Our goal should be to find that purpose and fulfill it.

Why are you here? Is it to evangelize and edify young people through your church's Sunday school program? Is it to assist family and friends as they serve on a foreign mission field? Is it to minister to those sick in the hospital or confined to a nursing home? Is it to visit the fatherless and widows, or the prisoners? If you don't know, ask God to show you. You can never be fulfilled as a Christian until you know what God saved you to do and then do it.

God's purpose gives life meaning.

Reflections/Prayer Requests

_____
_____
_____
_____
_____
_____

DAY 20

1 Kings 19:10

So he said, "I have been very zealous for the L<small>ORD</small> God of hosts; for the children of Israel have forsaken Your covenant, torn down Your altars, and killed Your prophets with the sword. I alone am left; and they seek to take my life."

I Alone Am Left

Upon returning from one of his globe-encircling voyages, Sir Francis Drake, the great explorer, anchored his ship in the little Thames River. A dangerous storm arose and it seemed that his ship would flounder. Someone standing near the old, weather-beaten seaman heard him say through gritted teeth, "Must I who have escaped the rage of the ocean be drowned in a ditch?"

Often a Christian who has withstood the assaults of Satan in severe trials and temptations falters because of a minor difficulty. Elijah found himself in such a position. He had confronted Ahab, king of Israel. He had stood up to 450 prophets of Baal. He had challenged the people of Israel to renew their commitment to the Lord. Then he was faced with the wrath of a vengeful woman, Jezebel. Not only did he flee, but he also began to feel sorry for himself. He concluded, "I alone am left; and they seek to take my life."

When we focus on the negative aspects of our situation, it's easy to slip into self-pity. Life is filled with many hardships and injustices. But as Elijah was about to learn, God's people are never left alone. God has promised not to keep us from the valleys, but to walk through them with us (Ps. 23:4). He has promised us not the absence of problems, but the guarantee of His presence (Heb. 13:5).

If you fall victim to self-pity, don't allow yourself to stay bogged down there. Whatever your circumstances, God is with you. The two of you together are sufficient for any situation.

You are never left alone when you are alone with God.

Reflections/Prayer Requests

DAY 21

1 Kings 19:11-12

Then He said, "Go out, and stand on the mountain before the L{\scriptsize ORD}." And behold, the L{\scriptsize ORD} passed by, and a great and strong wind tore into the mountains and broke the rocks in pieces before the L{\scriptsize ORD}, but the L{\scriptsize ORD} was not in the wind; and after the wind an earthquake, but the L{\scriptsize ORD} was not in the earthquake; and after the earthquake a fire, but the L{\scriptsize ORD} was not in the fire; and after the fire a still small voice.

Blessed Quietness

Years ago when people had ice boxes instead of refrigerators, a man working in an ice plant lost a valuable watch in the sawdust in which the ice was stored. His fellow workmen searched with him, but were unable to find it. They left the plant for lunch and returned to find a young boy with the watch. When they inquired how he found it, the boy replied, "I just lay down in the sawdust and heard it ticking." With all the noisy machinery turned off and a person predisposed to listen, the watch wasn't hard to find at all.

As Elijah stood on Mount Horeb, he was treated to a spectacular display of God's power. A great wind reduced mighty boulders to pebbles. An earthquake shook the ground. Then the mountain was bathed in fire. Each of these was a manifestation of God's power, but they were not God. It was not until all the noise had stopped that Elijah found God Himself—in a still, small voice.

Today it's hard to get away from the noise. The hubbub of the city, the noise of the factory, the cry of children, the blare of the radio or television—all contribute to a cacophony. In the midst of these things, intimate communion with God is nearly impossible. That's why it's essential that we seek a quiet retreat where we can hear God's still, small voice.

Find a place today where you can shut out the noise of the world. Ask God to calm your mind and remove the clamor that so often fills it. Tune your heart to listen for His voice and discover His intimacy. Get alone. Be still. Stay quiet. Hear God.

Intimacy with God comes in whispers, not shouts.

Reflections/Prayer Requests

_____

_____

_____

_____

_____

_____

DAY 22

1 Kings 19:15-16

*Then the L*ORD *said to him: "Go, return on your way to the Wilderness of Damascus; and when you arrive, anoint Hazael as king over Syria. Also you shall anoint Jehu the son of Nimshi as king over Israel. And Elisha the son of Shaphat of Abel Meholah you shall anoint as prophet in your place."*

Face Your Fears

Biologists say that fear is not only a universal emotion, but the first of the emotions to be developed in man and beast. If you have ever picked up a baby bird fallen from its nest, you have felt the rapid, terrified beating of its heart. Even though it has had no experience with you or any other person, it is fearful.

All of creation is under the dominion of fear. Man comes into this world stamped with fear before he is born, and those fears are multiplied as he increases in knowledge and experience. But it can be a mistake to make decisions based on fear.

Elijah made the mistake of giving in to his fears—and he fled from his homeland and his responsibilities. But when he renewed his commitment to God on Mount Horeb, the Lord turned him around and sent him back to face what he left behind. God knew the only way Elijah would conquer his fears was to confront them. Running away would never do it.

Many Christians have fled from their duties because of fears. Pastors have left churches, missionaries have come home from the field, mothers and fathers have left their families—all because of their fears: fear of failure, fear of pain, fear of suffering. But we can never overcome our fears if we have our back toward them, running away. We have to face them.

If you have allowed fear to cause you to flee from something you know you should do, turn around and face it. In God's power and by His will, you can have victory over your fears.

Never turn your back on your fears.

Reflections/Prayer Requests

_____
_____
_____
_____
_____
_____
_____
_____

DAY 23

1 Kings 19:18

"Yet I have reserved seven thousand in Israel, all whose knees have not bowed to Baal, and every mouth that has not kissed him."

All Is Not Lost

During the Boer War (1899-1902), a man was convicted of a very unusual crime. He was found guilty of being a "discourager." The South African town of Ladysmith was under attack, and this traitor would move up and down the lines of soldiers who were defending the city and do everything he could to discourage them. He would point out the enemy's strength, the difficulty of defending against them and the inevitable capture of the city. He didn't use a gun in his attack; it wasn't necessary. His weapon was the power of discouragement.

Satan is just such a discourager. He is not mentioned by name in this passage, but it's obvious he had disheartened Elijah. He convinced the prophet that all was lost. Over and over he told Elijah that "he alone was left." And Elijah came to believe that. But when it came time for Elijah to go back into the thick of things again, God revealed the truth to him. Instead of Satan's lie that "he alone was left," there were actually 7,000 people in Israel who had not followed after the false god Baal.

Satan is always ready to make things appear worse than they are if he can use it to discourage us. He continually tries to feed false information to believers so they might become discouraged, and too often he succeeds. God, however, offers the solution to Satan's lies—the exceeding great and precious promises of His Word. In the Bible we find more than enough optimism to overcome the Devil's pessimism.

If your life is filled with "doom and gloom," remember this may well be Satan's way of destroying your effectiveness for the Lord. How can you counter the Devil's devices? Turn to the promises of God's Word. Let the Bible be your encouragement today.

When God lifts you up, Satan can never put you down.

Reflections/Prayer Requests

DAY 24

1 Kings 19:19-21

So he departed from there, and found Elisha the son of Shaphat, who was plowing with twelve yoke of oxen before him, and he was with the twelfth. Then Elijah passed by him and threw his mantle on him. And he left the oxen and ran after Elijah, and said, "Please let me kiss my father and my mother, and then I will follow you." And he said to him, "Go back again, for what have I done to you?" So Elisha turned back from him, and took a yoke of oxen and slaughtered them and boiled their flesh, using the oxen's equipment, and gave it to the people, and they ate. Then he arose and followed Elijah, and served him.

No Turning Back

On December 21, 1620, the *Mayflower* dropped anchor in Plymouth Bay. It had been a grueling voyage across the Atlantic, taking the small ship 66 days to make the perilous crossing. There had been disease, anxiety and even childbirth among the 102 courageous passengers. Furthermore, they arrived on the bleak New England shore during a hard winter that ultimately claimed the lives of half their number. But when spring came and the captain of the *Mayflower* offered free passage to anyone desiring to return, not a single person accepted. These folks had made a commitment and they were not turning back.

Elijah's call to Elisha brought the same response. As a farmer, Elisha had been plowing with 12 yoke of oxen. When Elijah threw his mantle on this hardworking plowboy, Elisha took the very means of his livelihood, a yoke of oxen, and slaughtered them to provide a farewell feast for his friends. In doing so, he cut the ties to his old life and demonstrated his commitment to the ministry ahead of him.

Christians need to take this same step of commitment. We cannot live effectively for Christ if one foot is in the faith and the other is in the world. We need to make a clean break with the past and live for the Lord.

If God has called you to a particular kind of service, commit yourself unreservedly to it. Let your past be the past. Put it behind you and move forward with God. There's no greater ingredient for success in serving God.

There's no room for turning around in Christ's service.

Reflections/Prayer Requests

_____
_____
_____
_____
_____

DAY 25

1 Kings 21:20-22

Then Ahab said to Elijah, "Have you found me, O my enemy?" And he answered, "I have found you, because you have sold yourself to do evil in the sight of the L<small>ORD</small>: 'Behold, I will bring calamity on you. I will take away your posterity, and will cut off from Ahab every male in Israel, both bond and free. I will make your house like the house of Jeroboam the son of Nebat, and like the house of Baasha the son of Ahijah, because of the provocation with which you have provoked Me to anger, and made Israel sin.'"

Blessed Enemy

Those who might be called our enemies can actually do us great service. Socrates noted that every man needs a faithful friend and a bitter enemy—the one to advise him, and the other to make him look about him. Benjamin Franklin said, "Love your enemies, for they tell you your faults." And the Greek philosopher Antisthenes admonished, "Pay attention to your enemies, for they are the first to discover your mistakes."

Elijah could have helped King Ahab to discover his mistakes, if the king would have permitted him to do so. Ahab was surrounded by false prophets who were telling him only what they thought he wanted to hear. His wife, Jezebel, was leading him down the path of destruction by her zealous attempt to establish Baal worship in Israel. Elijah was his only hope, but the king dismissed him because he was an "enemy."

If a Christian is living for the Lord, he will have enemies. This will not be because he has cultivated them; it's simply the natural response of the world to the Gospel. But such a situation can be turned to our advantage. The Lord can use even our enemies to accomplish His will in our lives.

If you have an enemy, listen to him or her carefully. See if underneath their bitterness or anger there might not be a grain of truth in their complaint with you. Enemies often identify our faults much better than our friends do. Why not try listening to them? It may in the long run make you more Christlike.

Cherish your enemies; they may be blessings in disguise.

Reflections/Prayer Requests

_____
_____
_____
_____
_____
_____

DAY 26

2 Kings 1:2-3

Now Ahaziah fell through the lattice of his upper room in Samaria, and was injured; so he sent messengers and said to them, "Go, inquire of Baal-Zebub, the god of Ekron, whether I shall recover from this injury." But the angel of the LORD said to Elijah the Tishbite, "Arise, go up to meet the messengers of the king of Samaria, and say to them, 'Is it because there is no God in Israel that you are going to inquire of Baal-Zebub, the god of Ekron?'"

Is There No God?

Shortly after the outspoken atheist Robert G. Ingersoll was defeated in his race for governor of Illinois, he was spouting off about his atheism on board a train from Chicago to Peoria. He turned to a gentleman near him and demanded, "Tell me one great result that Christianity has ever accomplished." Not wishing to get into an argument with the boaster, the man hesitated to answer. For a moment it was silent in the car. Then an elderly lady who sat right behind him touched his arm with a trembling hand and said, "Sir, I do not know who you are, but I think I can tell you of one glorious thing which Christianity has done." "What is it, Madam?" asked Ingersoll. "It has kept Robert G. Ingersoll from being governor of the State of Illinois," she replied.

Those who choose to deny God always pay a great price. When King Ahaziah was injured and sent a messenger to inquire of the god of Ekron concerning his recovery, God sent Elijah to respond. "Because you have failed to trust the Lord," Elijah proclaimed, "you will die." And he did (v. 17). Ahaziah's unbelief cost him his life.

Unbelievers are not the only ones who stand to lose from their lack of faith. Christians sometimes profess to believe in Christ, but their actions fail to demonstrate they truly trust Him. Such inconsistency will cost them dearly in terms of peace and joy. It could even cause them to lose some of their heavenly rewards.

Let your walk match your talk. If you trust the Lord for your salvation, trust Him for all the other areas of your life as well. When you get God's counsel, you've got the best counsel there is.

Unbelief is never cheap; it costs more than it pays.

Reflections/Prayer Requests

_____
_____
_____
_____
_____
_____

DAY 27

2 Kings 1:10-12

So Elijah answered and said to the captain of fifty, "If I am a man of God, then let fire come down from heaven and consume you and your fifty men." And fire came down from heaven and consumed him and his fifty. Then he sent to him another captain of fifty with his fifty men. And he answered and said to him: "Man of God, thus has the king said, 'Come down quickly!'" So Elijah answered and said to them, "If I am a man of God, let fire come down from heaven and consume you and your fifty men." And the fire of God came down from heaven and consumed him and his fifty.

God Takes Care of His Own

Many years ago on a bitterly cold January night, the inhabitants of the town of Sleswick, Germany, were in great distress. A hostile army was marching on them, and the reports of the conduct of these lawless soldiers struck fear in every resident's heart. In this town, however, lived a grandmother with her widowed daughter and her grandson. As they waited, this aged woman prayed for God to "build a wall of defense around them." At midnight the enemy came pouring into the village, breaking down the doors of the houses. But not even a knock came to this woman's door. In the morning she found out why. The snowfall that night had drifted in front of her door, creating such a massive wall that it was impossible to get to them. "There!" said the grandmother. "God answered my prayers. He raised up a wall around us!"

God does take care of His own. When King Ahaziah sent a regiment of 50 men and their captain to take Elijah by force, God responded to Elijah's predicament by sending down fire that consumed them. The same happened to a second group of 50. It was only when a third group approached Elijah with the fear of the Lord that their lives were spared.

Every Christian walks under the protective watch care of an omnipotent God. There is not a moment when His eye is not on us. Take heart. Until God's purpose for you on earth is completed, no danger can truly threaten you. God will take care of you.

Fear God and you'll have nothing else to fear.

Reflections/Prayer Requests

_____
_____
_____
_____
_____
_____

DAY 28

2 Kings 2:1-2

And it came to pass, when the LORD was about to take up Elijah into heaven by a whirlwind, that Elijah went with Elisha from Gilgal. Then Elijah said to Elisha, "Stay here, please, for the LORD has sent me on to Bethel." And Elisha said, "As the LORD lives, and as your soul lives, I will not leave you!" So they went down to Bethel.

Step-by-step

A man was driving along a highway when he suddenly ran into a stretch of dense fog. While considering how he might stay on the road, he noticed a reflector light along the shoulder of the road catching the glare of his headlights. Slowly he inched himself up to the first reflector only to discover that a second reflector light was now showing in the distance. When he reached the second, he found a third shining up ahead. Slowly, light by light, he worked his way along the highway until he drove out of the fog.

As Elijah traveled toward his ultimate meeting with the Lord, he found that God led him in the same way. First he was instructed to leave Gilgal and go to Bethel. From Bethel he was led to Jericho (v. 4); from Jericho he was led to the Jordan River (v. 6) and on into the wilderness (v. 11). God did not reveal the whole journey beforehand, but led the prophet step-by-step along the way.

So often we Christians want to know what's ahead for us and our loved ones. We chafe because God doesn't reveal His plans for next week or next month or next year. But God is much more interested in developing our trust than He is in revealing the future. His light is always sufficient for the next step, but seldom for the entire trip.

Let God lead you step-by-step. Trust that as He has given you enough light to take the next step, He will continue to provide for each step along the way. Be content with God's provision for today and let the future rest with Him.

God won't light your second step until you have taken the first one.

Reflections/Prayer Requests

_____
_____
_____
_____
_____
_____
_____
_____

DAY 29

2 Kings 2:6-8

Then Elijah said to him, "Stay here, please, for the LORD has sent me on to the Jordan." But he said, "As the LORD lives, and as your soul lives, I will not leave you!" So the two of them went on. And fifty men of the sons of the prophets went and stood facing them at a distance, while the two of them stood by the Jordan. Now Elijah took his mantle, rolled it up, and struck the water; and it was divided this way and that, so that the two of them crossed over on dry ground.

Let Your Light Still Shine

Serving the Lord is not just for the young. John Wesley preached until he died at age 90. Gladys Stall of Lake Magdalene, Florida, has taught Sunday school for 82 years. She began at the age of 14 and is still teaching six-and seven-year-olds at the age of 96.

As we encounter Elijah in the last few days of his ministry, we find a man still actively proclaiming the reality and glory of God. Proceeding toward his appointment with destiny and the fiery chariot of God, he demonstrated the power of God by parting the water of the Jordan. Even in his closing moments, Elijah dramatically revealed that the God of Israel is an awesome God.

Christians never reach the age where they can completely "retire" from the Lord's service. Even when we may physically no longer be able to do the things we once did, God can still use us to reveal His power and glory. It may be in a ministry of prayer or encouragement, and that may prove to be the best ministry we've ever had. Perhaps God will demonstrate His awesome power through the life experiences of His more senior saints. However He chooses, our latter years should be as much at His disposal as our former ones.

Whatever you have left in this life, give it to God. Commit yourself to bring glory to Him in your elder years as you have in your younger ones. Who knows? The best may be yet to come.

*** Finishing well brings more glory to God than beginning well.***

Reflections/Prayer Requests

_____

_____

_____

_____

_____

_____

_____

DAY 30

2 Kings 2:1, 11

And it came to pass, when the LORD was about to take up Elijah into heaven by a whirlwind, that Elijah went with Elisha from Gilgal. Then it happened, as they continued on and talked, that suddenly a chariot of fire appeared with horses of fire, and separated the two of them; and Elijah went up by a whirlwind into heaven.

In the Midst of the Whirlwind

Eagles have an interesting flight pattern. Instead of fleeing the winds of stormy weather, they turn to face them. The same winds that blow others away are used by these magnificent birds to lift them higher.

A storm lifted Elijah into the presence of God. Traveling from Gilgal with his disciple Elisha, he was forewarned by the sons of the prophets in Bethel, and again in Jericho, that this was the day God would take him away. But instead of fleeing from this potentially frightening possibility, the prophet continued on, content to let God have His will. When they crossed over the Jordan River, a chariot of fire separated Elisha from his master, and a whirlwind lifted Elijah up and away. The roaring winds of a desert storm, which normally brought destruction, became for Elijah the vehicle by which God elevated him into heaven.

When life's whirlwinds blow through our lives, we have a choice. We can focus on our trials and troubles, or we can use the whirlwind to be lifted up before the Lord in prayer and praise. What others see as a deadly devastation can become that which draws us more completely into God's presence.

Don't run away from the storms of life. They may be God's method of bringing you closer to Him. Instead, spread your wings of prayer and praise. Consider the winds of strife as opportunities to be lifted closer to the Lord.

Don't let your trials blow you down; let them lift you up.

Reflections/Prayer Requests

_____
_____
_____
_____
_____
_____
_____
_____
_____

DAY 31

2 Kings 2:14

Then he took the mantle of Elijah that had fallen from him, and struck the water, and said, "Where is the LORD God of Elijah?" And when he also had struck the water, it was divided this way and that; and Elisha crossed over.

In His Steps

Someone once said, "The footsteps that a boy usually wants to follow are those that his father hoped he had covered up." But not so with Elijah.

In the time that Elijah had spent with Elisha, he left behind footprints that he hoped his "spiritual son" would be able and willing to follow. Not the least of these was the miraculous way God demonstrated His power through his prophet. Just as the Lord had parted the water of the Jordan River when Elijah struck it with his mantle (v. 8), Elisha soon discovered that God would do the same for him as he walked in Elijah's footsteps.

Every Christian leaves behind footprints. As he walks through the good times as well as times of difficulty, and as he demonstrates God's power and presence in the various situations he encounters as a believer, a Christian leaves indelible impressions upon those who are watching.

If people were to follow in your footsteps, where would they be led? Would they find themselves at places of pleasure more often than at church? Would your footprints lead to questionable activities rather than to godly behavior? Would they discover more intimacy with God because they trod where you had stepped?

As you make your way through life, remember that others are coming behind you. Be sure your feet only take you where you want their feet to take them. Like it or not, you're leaving footprints behind that they will want to follow.

Watch where you step; those you love are close behind.

Reflections/Prayer Requests

_____

_____

_____

_____

_____

_____

_____

_____

GIANTS OF THE OLD TESTAMENT

Look for these other titles in the series:

Lessons on Living From Moses

Lessons on Living From Esther

Lessons on Living From Isaiah

Lessons on Living From Joshua

Lessons on Living From Abraham

Also coming in 1998:

Lessons on Living From Ruth

Lessons on Living From Jeremiah

Lessons on Living From David

Lessons on Living From Solomon

Lessons on Living From Daniel

Lessons on Living From Job

Lessons on Living From Joseph